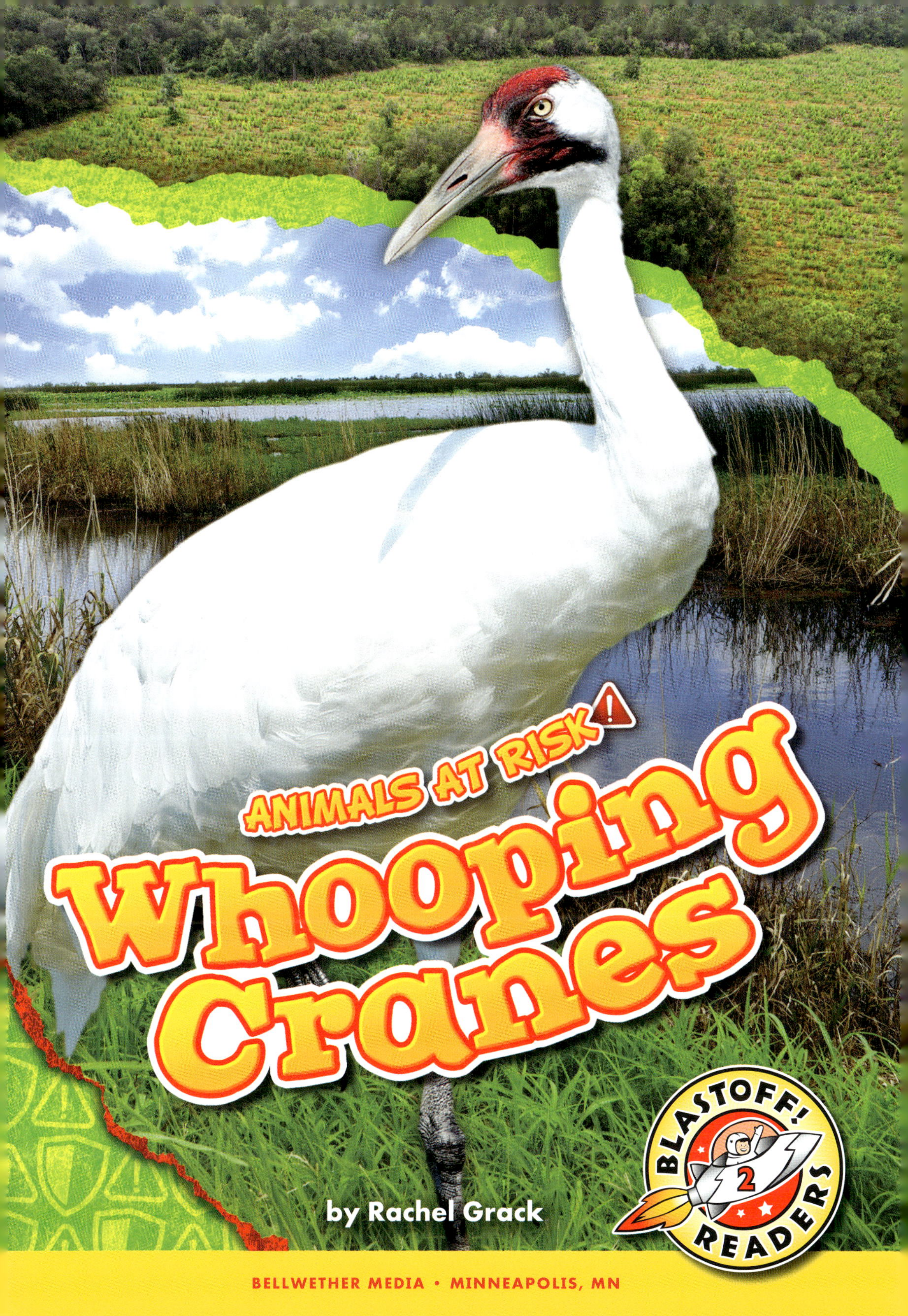
ANIMALS AT RISK
Whooping Cranes
by Rachel Grack
BLASTOFF! 2 READERS
BELLWETHER MEDIA • MINNEAPOLIS, MN

Blastoff! Readers are carefully developed by literacy experts to build reading stamina and move students toward fluency by combining standards-based content with developmentally appropriate text.

Level 1 provides the most support through repetition of high-frequency words, light text, predictable sentence patterns, and strong visual support.

Level 2 offers early readers a bit more challenge through varied sentences, increased text load, and text-supportive special features.

Level 3 advances early-fluent readers toward fluency through increased text load, less reliance on photos, advancing concepts, longer sentences, and more complex special features.

★ **Blastoff! Universe**

Reading Level

Grade K

Grades 1–3

Grade 4

This edition first published in 2025 by Bellwether Media, Inc.

Library of Congress Cataloging-in-Publication Data

LC record for Whooping Cranes available at: https://lccn.loc.gov/2024009417

Editor: Kieran Downs   Designer: Brittany McIntosh

Printed in the United States of America, North Mankato, MN.

Table of Contents

Tall Fliers

Whooping cranes are the tallest birds in North America! They stand on long, thin legs.

They are white with black wingtips. The tops of their heads are red.

Many whooping cranes once filled the skies. They **migrated** across North America.

Today, they are **endangered**. People have caused most of their problems.

In Danger!

Whooping cranes nest in **wetlands**. But people fill their **habitats** with dirt for farms.

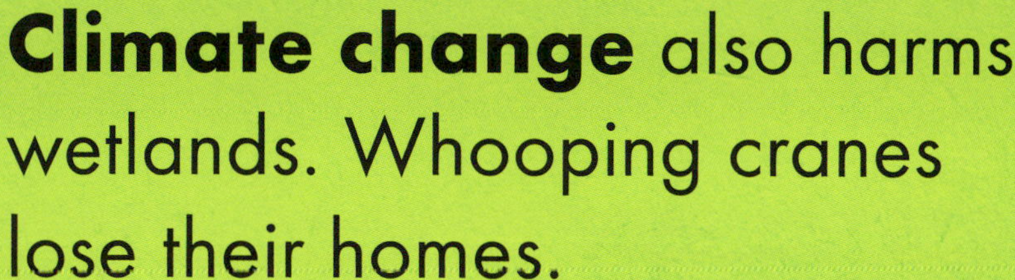

Climate change also harms wetlands. Whooping cranes lose their homes.

Threats

1 people need farmland

2 wetlands are filled with dirt

3 whooping cranes lose homes

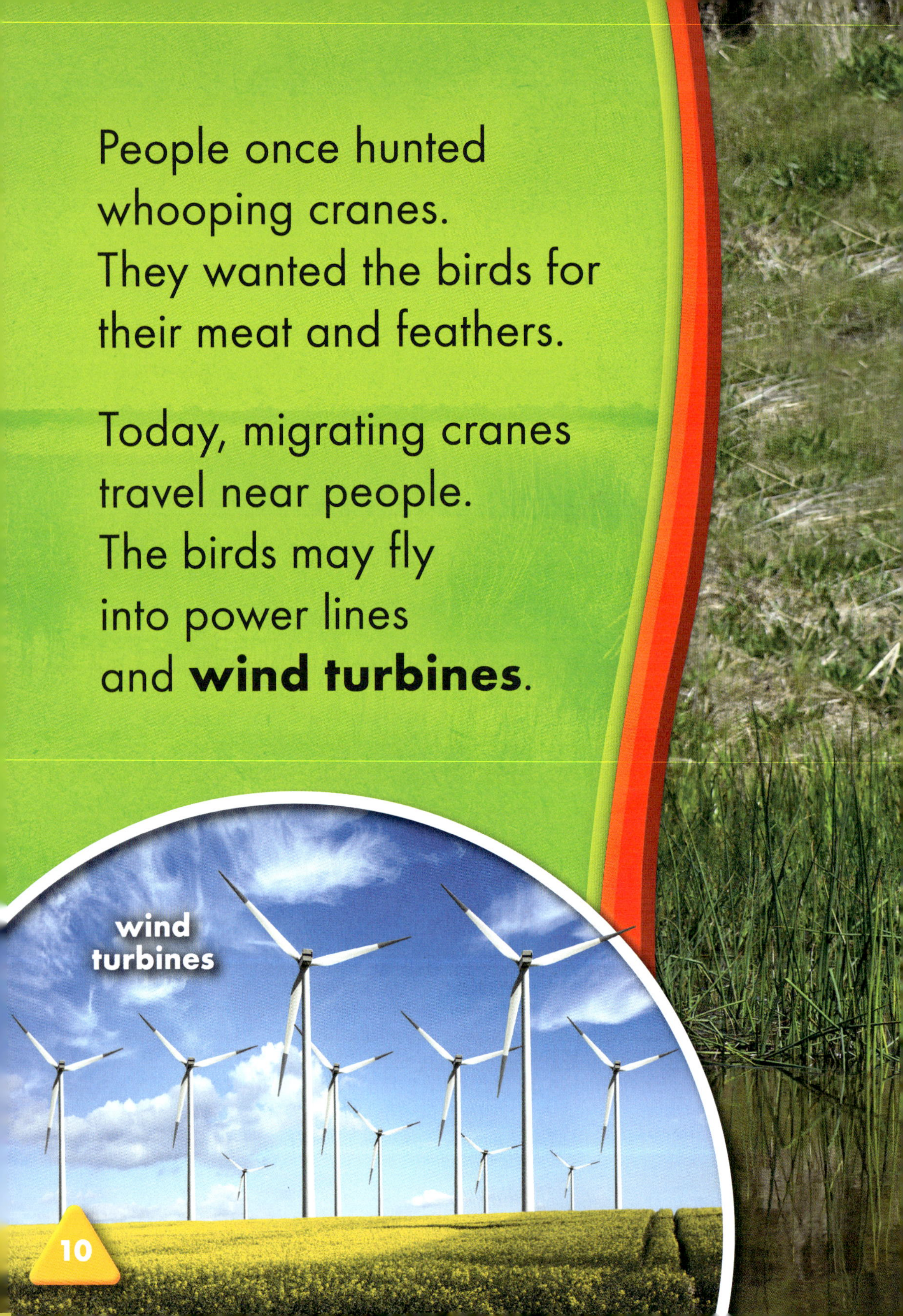

People once hunted whooping cranes. They wanted the birds for their meat and feathers.

Today, migrating cranes travel near people. The birds may fly into power lines and **wind turbines**.

Whooping Crane Stats

Least Concern	Near Threatened	Vulnerable	Endangered	Critically Endangered	Extinct in the Wild	Extinct

conservation status: endangered

life span: up to 30 years

Save the Whooping Cranes!

Whooping cranes keep wetlands healthy. They are important to the **food chain**.

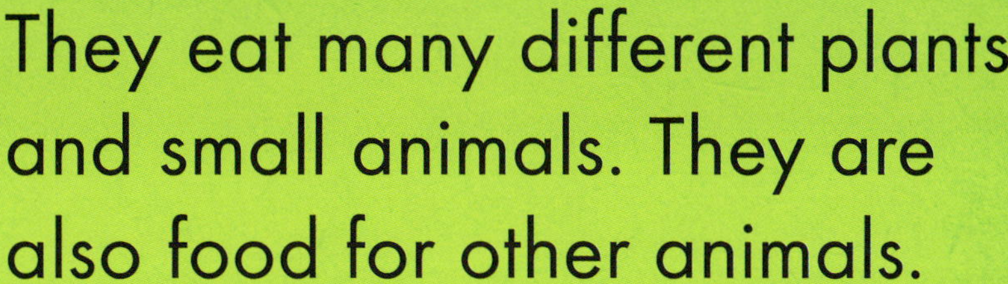
They eat many different plants and small animals. They are also food for other animals.

The World with Whooping Cranes

more whooping cranes

healthy food chain

healthy wetlands

Governments set aside land for whooping cranes. They pass **laws** against hunting them.

People **protect** wetlands along **migration paths**.

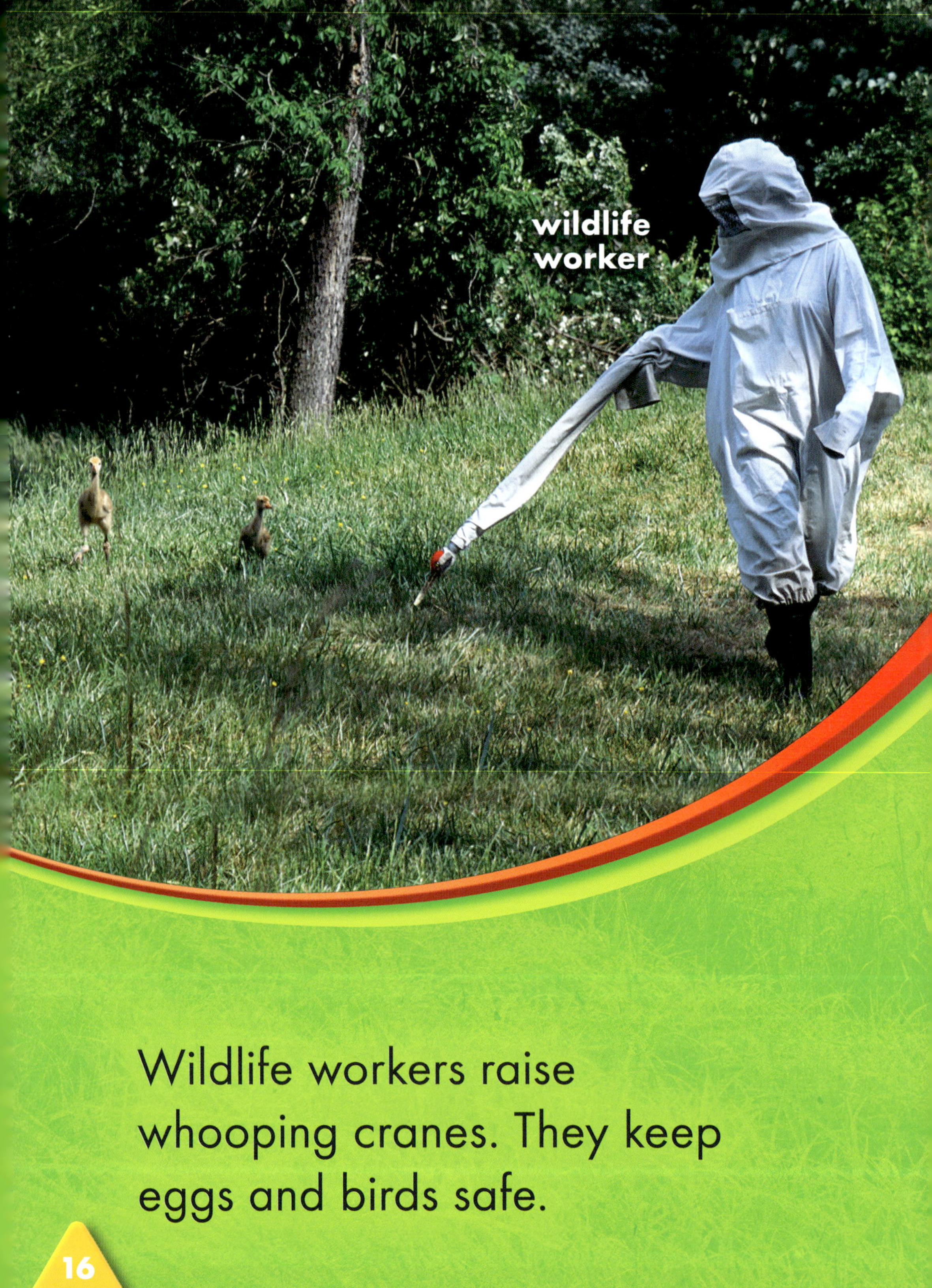

Wildlife workers raise whooping cranes. They keep eggs and birds safe.

They take in hurt birds. They return healthy birds to the wild.

People teach young whooping cranes where to migrate.

They fly planes with the birds. They lead the birds to safe stopping spots.

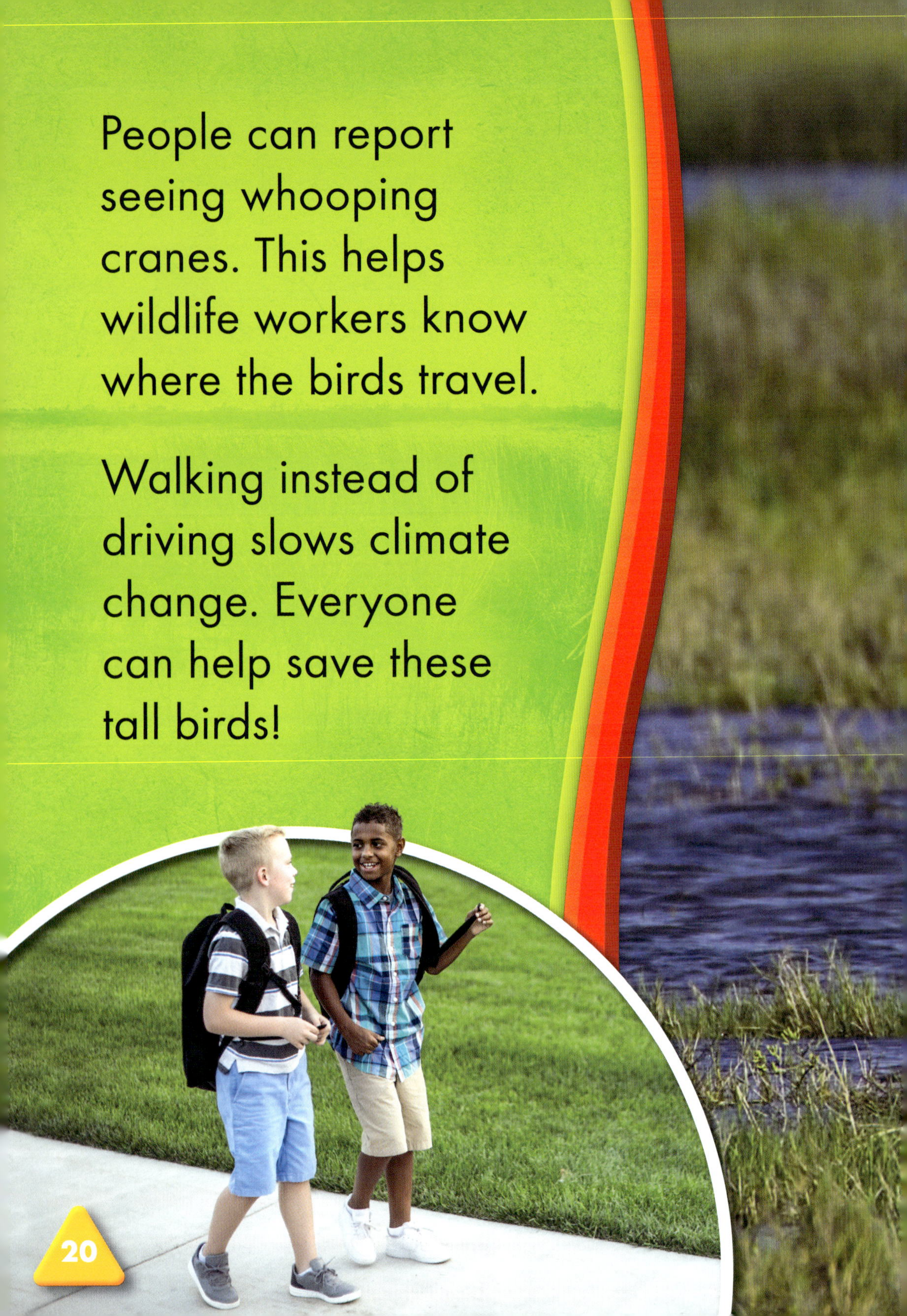

People can report seeing whooping cranes. This helps wildlife workers know where the birds travel.

Walking instead of driving slows climate change. Everyone can help save these tall birds!

Glossary

climate change—a human-caused change in Earth's weather due to warming temperatures

endangered—in danger of dying out

food chain—a system of who eats what

habitats—the places where animals live

laws—rules that must be followed

migrated—traveled from one place to another, often with the seasons

migration paths—pathways used to travel from one place to another, often with the seasons

protect—to keep safe

wetlands—areas of land that are covered with low levels of water for most of the year

wind turbines—machines that turn wind into electrical energy

To Learn More

AT THE LIBRARY

Amstutz, Lisa. *Cranes.* Mankato, Minn.: Amicus, 2023.

Huddleston, Emma. *Whooping Cranes.* Minneapolis, Minn.: Bearport Publishing Company, 2023.

Sabelko, Rebecca. *Wetlands.* Minneapolis, Minn.: Bellwether Media, 2022.

ON THE WEB

FACTSURFER

Factsurfer.com gives you a safe, fun way to find more information.

1. Go to www.factsurfer.com.

2. Enter "whooping cranes" into the search box and click 🔍.

3. Select your book cover to see a list of related content.

Index

The images in this book are reproduced through the courtesy of: Joe Ferrer, front cover, p. 3; Mathew Cowger, front cover (tear), p. 3; critterbiz, pp. 4, 10-11; Jack Nevitt, p. 5; Dennis W Donohue, p. 6; Irina Mos, p. 8; Bilanol, p. 9 (left); Eric Buermeyer, p. 9 (right); Tony Campbell, p. 9 (bottom); majeczka, p. 10; Gabbro/ Alamy, p. 12; William Cushman, p. 13 (left); Jay Connors, p. 13 (right); Oleksandr Koretskyi, p. 13 (bottom); Danae Abreu, p. 14; Agnieszka Bacal, p. 15; Mark Payne-Gill, p. 16; The Washington Post/ Contributor/ Getty, p. 17; Janice and Nolan Braud/ Alamy, p. 18; Danita Delimont, p. 19; Brocreative, p. 20; Richard Seeley, pp. 20-21; Connie Barr, p. 23.